CREATIVE IKEBANA

CREATIVE

Ikebana

a new way with flowers

NORIKO OHNO

JAPAN PUBLICATIONS, INC.

FOREWORD

Wherever one goes in the world there are beautiful flowers. People everywhere enjoy arranging flowers and admiring them as part of their intimate lives. Since doing so is only human, there is no reason why ikebana should have rigid sets of rules which one dare not trespass.

Convinced of the truth of this attitude and painfully aware that the fracture of ikebana itself into warring schools of thought could spell the corruption of the art, I established the International Ikebana Association (Kokusai Ikebana Kyōkai). My aim in doing so was not merely to promote flower-arranging gatherings of peoples in many lands. I wanted, while maintaining our pride in the Japanese tradition of ikebana, to surpass the narrow bounds of "school" to develop ikebana into a worldwide art that respects individuality and expresses creative modernity. In this way I think we can make a total art of ikebana and, through it, contribute to world cultural exchange.

International ikebana can fuse with our daily lives. It can create an international appreciation of flower arranging that assimilates traditional Japanese ikebana and expands its bonds to include the color schemes, flowers, and vases of all countries.

Though highly ornamental Western floral art uses blossoms as design material only, the Japanese attitude is a deeper, more spiritual one. International ikebana emphasizes individual creative powers; it puts the individual first. All human faces and forms are different. Similarly, what is inside each individual differs from what is inside each other. Though we might all feel the beauty of a rose, we all feel it in different ways. Our task is to bring into the world of ikebana particular differences in feeling toward beauty and express them through flowers.

We do not rely on strict forms but prefer to avoid becoming bogged down and to permit free alterations of the numbers of flowers, leaves, or branches one uses and to allow one to arrange freely the angles at which the individual branches stand. This lets the arranger savor fully the wonderful joy of ikebana.

Another important aspect of the art is to give reign to the individuality of the flowers one uses. When we speak of individual expression we mean that of the flowers as well as that of the person doing the arranging.

However wonderful a flower arrangement, it is lost if it fails to suit the place in which it is displayed. Only when arrangement, vase, and place of display become one is the total art of ikebana born.

The foundation of a study of international ikebana is a deepening of one's sensitivity through appreciation of the beauty of nature and that of good works of art. Ikebana demands that one know flowers and humbly study their ways of life.

CONTENTS

TELEVISION IN AMSTERDAM

In 1968, invited by Princess Grace to be one of
twelve judges in the Monte Carlo Florae exhibit,
on my return trip, I visited fourteen countries
including France, Holland, Poland, Czechoslovakia, Hungary, Switzerland, Turkey, Lebanon,
Iraq, and Taiwan and gave twenty ikebana
demonstrations. This photograph is from a
television program from Amsterdam.

SUMMER FESTIVAL

Materials: raspberry leaves, Japanese lanterns, dried ferns
Container: clay vase with two openings

MARC CHAGALL

In his lovely home on top of an olive-covered hill overlooking
the Mediterranean, Marc Chagall arranged yellow mimosa,
and thistles in a large glass vase and placed them in front of
his masterpiece "Amore" with the joyful exclamation, "It *is*
the South of France!"

Marcel Marceau

"Flowers are fragile, brittler than anything. Petals flutter at the touch of a finger; they are always at the breaking point, and I love them for it." Marceau's answers to my questions about flowers sang as a chanson. I gave him a white vase with a few red roses, and he said, "Japanese ikebana is wonderful. It maintains a new order filled with the voice of living blossoms. For this reason I consider it a sort of pantomime." He then walked on the stage and performed a beautiful pantomime for me about flowers and people. I was deeply moved.

WATER POEM

Materials: water lily caladium leaf, glass balls
Container: tri-color glass vase

CHRISTMAS FANTASY *Materials:* palm leaf, bleached yam vines, white anthurium, ginger flower, silver tinsel, red candle
Container: white, unglazed double-mouth vase

INTRODUCTION

Ikebana, the Japanese art of arranging flowers, has a long history. The famous eleventh-century miscellany *Makura no Sōshi* (*The Pillow Book*) mentions "cherry blossoms in a celadon vase," and the diaries of the Kamakura period (1185–1333) speak of flowers arranged for the July festival of the stars, the Tanabata. The actual art of ikebana traditionally dates from the Muromachi period (1392–1568). This was an age most famous for the widespread wrangling among the power holders of the nation and the warfare that laid Kyoto, the seat of most of the country's culture, in ashes. It was also, however, an age when the arts developed lively and exciting new forms. Ikebana, one of those new developments, ceased being merely a way of arranging floral offerings (*kuge*) to the Buddha and began to crystallize as an art form appreciated for itself. *Tatebana,* a then fashionable elaborate flower arrangement style, better known by the name *rikka,* shared the seat of honor with a special brand of *tatebana* simultaneously developing in the Imperial Court.

Townspeople, then rapidly growing in financial power, as well as the court nobles, arranged flower meets to demonstrate their prowess. These meets gradually grew into associations, the forebears of the now famous ikebana schools. Though the skill of the arrangers of the period must have been marvelous, technique is not the heart of the Japanese fondness for the floral art. Nature is a very important aspect of all phases of Japanese life. The people of Japan see in mountains, trees, blades of grass, and the humblest flowers a kind of divinity. An aura of mystic love of nature has always surrounded the Japanese devotion to flowers and has resulted in the distinctively spiritual nature of ikebana. As ikebana grew into a full-fledged art, attention in it tended to shift from the flowers themselves to the arrangers.

With the passing of time, as the *rikka* style grew more and more gorgeous, the famous tea ceremony came into fashion. For the purposes of this refined and subtle cult, the flowery majesties of the *rikka* were unsuitable. Another style was needed, and the tea masters themselves invented it: the charming and simple *nageire* also known as *chabana,* or tea flowers. The main aim of these simple arrangement was to recreate the feeling flowers have when growing in the field. The soft and elegant tastes of the tea ceremony gained in popularity and with them so did the *nageire* style which soon demanded simple, rough vases of exquisite coloration to replace the elaborate painted porcelain affairs previously in mode. Baskets made of bamboo and fitted with containers for water made superb tea-ceremony flower containers, as we can tell from the famous flower basket now kept in the temple Onjō-ji and attributed to the most famous of all the tea masters, Sen no Rikyū.

Gradually, with the passing ages, ikebana developed into an ornamental and artistic form so deeply infused with the typical Japanese love of beauty and Nature, that flower arranging is today, and will always be, an accomplishment much treasured by our entire nation.

Unfortunately, as ikebana grew and developed certain fixed techniques and forms, a number of strict schools of doctrine developed, codified their notions on the subject of floral arrangement, and atrophied into formidable and rigid rules that tolerate no transgression. I feel that rules of this sort are not only unnecessary but that they are also harmful to the natural and fruitful growth of a living art. Creation is the key to all art, including ikebana. I hope that what I have written in this book and the arrangements I have made to illustrate my points will prove of value to all those seeking an understanding of the heart, not just the body, of living creative ikebana.

Chapter One
Basics

PURPOSE OF THE CHAPTER

To begin in any art or craft, one must acquire a knowledge of the materials and tools and must familiarize oneself thoroughly with the basic styles and forms that have made up the background of the art or craft. I do not mean that we are about to launch on a set of rigid rules that it is forbidden to transgress. I do mean that you must learn to crawl before you walk and walk before you run in ikebana as well as in anything else. You will find that I have set forth in this chapter a number of hints and suggestions that will give you a foundation from which to develop your own individual ideas with flowers and vases of your own selection. In later sections of the book, I have collected a number of my arrangements not for you to copy, but for you to use as grist in the mill of your own originality.

1. EQUIPMENT

The very minimum you will want are a pair of flower scissors, different, as you can tell, from ordinary scissors, and some *kenzan*, or wire-nail flower holders that keep the flowers and other materials where you want them. A number of other pieces of equipment, however, will prove very handy. You will find them explained in this chapter.

Scissors (*warabite*).

SCISSORS

The ones shown are called *warabite*, but any heavy pair of sturdy scissors, the bigger the better, and of course, the more comfortable the better, will do. From time to time, give your scissors a good coat of oil to keep them from rusting and gumming up with sap.

HATCHET, KNIFE, AND SAW

Use the hatchet and the knife when thick roots and branches defy scissors. The saw is useful for anything too big for the other tools to handle.

Hatchet.

Saw.

Knife.

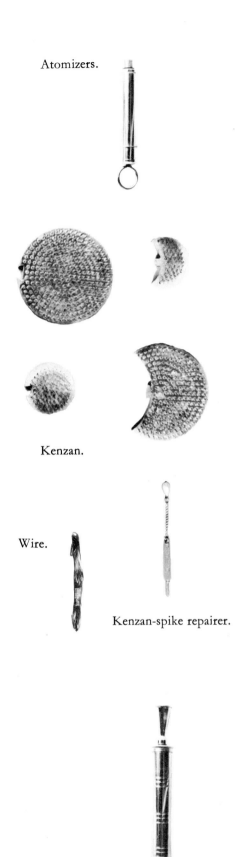

Atomizers.

Kenzan.

Wire.

Kenzan-spike repairer.

ATOMIZER

A fine mist of water adds greatly to the cooling value of an arrangement and prolongs the life of the materials. This piece of equipment, when fitted with a trumpet-shaped nozzle, is good for forcing water into the thick stalks of water lilies and lotus flowers.

KENZAN

There are a variety of shapes and sizes of kenzan used either separately or together. Be sure you select those that have closely packed, firmly set spikes and that are weighty enough to hold your materials in place.

KENZAN SPIKE REPAIRER

Nothing can take the place of this handy device when you find yourself having to straighten the bent spikes of a kenzan.

WIRE

Thin wire is useful in tying materials in place or sometimes for balling up and dropping into a tall vase to replace a kenzan.

SMALL STONES AND GRAVEL

Always have some gravel on hand to cover up the kenzan in low flat vases. You will find a little sand useful for special effects.

INJECTION PUMP

With an injection pump you can fill the stalks of hollow-stem materials.

2. VASES

The most important thing in selecting vases is to be sure that they always match the mood and colors of the flowers you are going to put in them. Also make sure the vase will harmonize with the room in which you intend to display your finished ikebana. In addition to true vases, you may also use other vessels for interesting variety. Whatever you use, however, remember that the choice of vase is almost as important as the choice of the flowers. Do not select heedlessly.

With vases that are warm in color, feel free to use any kind of flower or branch that matches. The most useful ikebana rule of thumb is that you must avoid one thing: flashy vases with flashy flowers. A simple vase makes gorgeous blossoms look much lovelier than a gaudy patterned one does. In all likelihood, you will use your vases over and over again. Do not choose faddy, unusual ones or overly decorative ones that you will tire of quickly.

COMPOTES

Though originally designed for fruits, compotes serve ikebana purposes well.

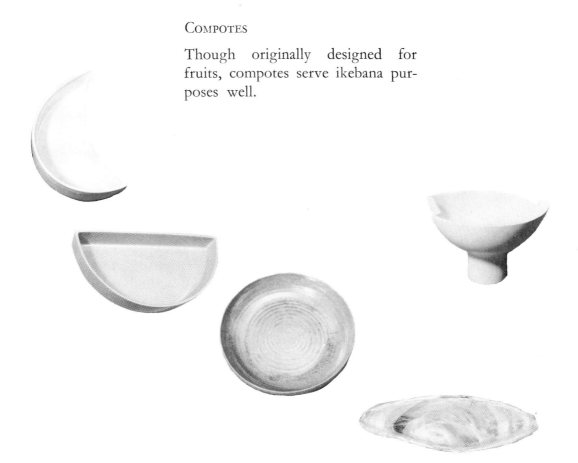

POTS

Pot- and jar-shaped vases require a little more skill in the handling than flat dishes. They are, however, frequently quite effective. Of the many kinds, some are too narrow in the mouth for a kenzan; in these cases use stones or a ball of wire to hold the materials in place.

BOTTLES

Informal arrangements of the *nageire* style frequently use bottle-shaped containers. We almost never use kenzan with these tall slender containers, but hold the materials in place with short sticks of wood firmly fitted inside the vase. Learning how to do this is a requisite to the use of this kind of container.

We have been talking mostly about ceramic vases of the true vase sort, but you can find around you any number of interesting things that, depending on the time and the place, will make wonderful flower containers. For instance, creels, rustic colanders, interesting bottles, salad bowls or large plates, beer steins, cut-glass bowls, hats, cookie jars, and many more. Keep your eye open all the time for the interesting object that has some intimate connection with you or your family. Remember, the important thing in selecting any king of vase is to be sure it harmonizes with both the flowers and the setting in question to create a beautiful and joy-giving work of art.

If you live where bamboo grows, you can have a lot of fun going out into the woods, cutting some, and converting it into vases that have a flavor of the Orient. A last hint, a simple black vase, like the basic black dress, is right on almost all occasions.

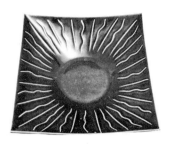

3. MATERIALS

Whatever materials you are buying, the following three rules hold true.

1. Select with care, and buy only as much as you need.
2. Buy from reputable dealers.
3. Take your materials home immediately, and take prompt steps to preserve them.

Most often, you will buy flowers or branches and leaves. Anything that fits the image you have in mind and that matches the setting will do. The following suggestions will help you decide whether to use one or more types of plant in an arrangement.

Generally, combine two or more kinds of plant in a single arrangement. You can, however, create some lovely special effects with a single kind such as camelias, daffodils, cherry boughs, iris, sweet flags, clematis, cosmos, or roses of one colors.

Remember that flowers rival each other in color and form; none of them creates the same color effect. When you combine them, whether you use warm or cool colors, use the same good sense you would in selecting accessories to go with your clothes. A woman will reveal her individuality by her fondness for cool colors or torrid, hot ones, but regardless of personal preferences, a certain good taste in combination must always prevail.

What is true for colors also holds for shapes. From the fantastic big leaves of the monstrosa and the flamboyant blossoms of the peony to the dainty leaves of the willow and the fragile blossoms of the peach everything is different in shape and requires certain other forms and shapes to bring out its best aspect. Select forms and colors that harmonize, and use your eye to work magic in blending and contrasting shape and shape, color and color, line and line.

Combining kinds of flowers results in a beauty impossible with only one sort. When you buy flowers or cut them from your garden, do so with an eye to what will go with what. The following guide lines will be helpful:

1. Flowers and Boughs

This is one of the easiest and loveliest combinations. Select, for instance, pine and roses, rape blossoms and flowering peach boughs, tulips and pussy willow.

2. Green Leaves and Bright Flowers

The green of maiden hair fern, asparagus, monstrosa, fatsia, cycads, and ferns harmonizes beautifully with such brilliant blooms as roses, carnations, tulips, peonies, African daisies, rhododendron, hydrangeas, dahlias, or crysanthemums.

3. Two or Three Kinds of Spray Flowers

Long sprays of two or three different kinds like patrinia or gentians are unusually effective.

DRIED MATERIALS

In addition to the many varieties of everlastings, wood roses, chestnuts, and other dried materials commercially available, you will find a new thrill in arranging for autumn and winter if you go into the woods and fields and gather armfuls of berries and grasses yourself, bring them home, and dry them for future use. There is a distinctive elegance and beauty in arrangements of dried materials that people all over the world seem to appreciate.

OTHER NATURAL MATERIALS

Combinations of vegetables, vines, fruits, roots, driftwood, pieces of logs, gourds, pumpkins, berries, and many more colorful or somber articles make appealing arrangements and table centerpieces.

ARTIFICIAL MATERIALS

Sometimes, for show windows or exhibitions it is necessary to use materials that last longer than natural flowers and branches. Feathers, plastics, wood, steel wire, and glass are often effective, but natural materials are always more emotionally satisfying than artificial ones. For long-lasting displays try dried, bleached, or otherwise processed natural materials first.

4. TRIMMING TECHNIQUES

Slip the top handle of the scissors over your thumb, and rest it well down on the base in the crotch between your thumb and your index finger. The bottom handle should rest in the bend of your other four fingers. The cutting action comes from closing your entire hand, not from your fingertips alone. The scissors will be difficult to use if they are either too stiff or too loose. Always apply a firm, steady grip. Though some people put their index finger in the handle to cut, this in fact only reduces the power your cut generates. The quickest way to master good cutting techniques is to think of hanging the scissors on your thumb and using the rest of your hand to do the work.

Judicious Trimming

1. Flowers

Though in nature a profusion of blooms is lovely, for arrangements we must select just those flowers that create the mood or effect we want. First, clip away all withered or crushed blossoms; next carefully examine the material, and trim away everything but the flowers you know will contribute to the desired effect.

If you are going to use a kenzan, you will have to cut fleshy stem plants at right angles. Cutting them on a diagonal increases the area of the opening and correspondingly the ability of the stalk to take in water. This is fine if your arrangement is one for a deep vase in which you will not require a kenzan, but if you do use one, the diagonal cut results in a fragile end that split on the kenzan points.

Do not chop flower stems. Give them a clean cut.

2. Leaves

Cut leaves to accent strengths in the lines and colors. Select the ones you will leave on the branch with a careful eye to the beauty of the individual plant's characteristics. Be sure that you use only the leaves that will play a vital part in your arrangement. In ikebana there is no room for non-essentials.

3. Branches

Trimming branches enlivens by abbreviating and improving the natural materials. Do not be timid. Clip away unwanted branches with a bold hand, and your arrangements are sure to be much lovelier. Cut at forks only. Cutting midway a branch leaves unsightly scars and debris. If you must leave a scar in a branch either by cutting away a large leaf or by cutting midway, hide it by tinting the opening with India ink.

5. FOUR THINGS TO REMEMBER

A. Woody or fleshy stems, for which you will not use a kenzan, should be cut diagonally to increase the materials' water intake.

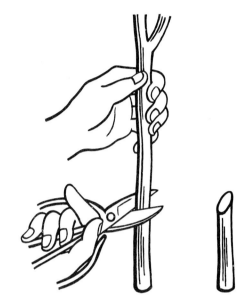

Fig. 1. Cutting on an angle.

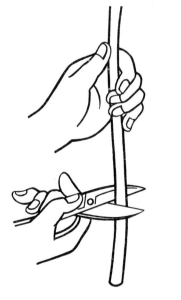

B. Fleshy stems to be used with a kenzan must be cut straight across, or they will lack sufficient strength to stand on the kenzan points.

Fig. 2. Cutting horizontally.

C. Cut all materials under water to make them last longer.

Fig. 3. Cutting under water.

D. Soften the bottoms of woody materials by making a few cuts (see illustration). They will then stand better on the kenzan.

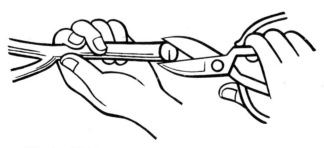

Fig. 4. Making slits in the cut end of the stalk.

6. BENDING

SLITTING AND BENDING

Some thick woody stalks and branches offer so much resistance that it is difficult to bend them using the basic method, but reckless use of the knife weakens them and makes them easy to break. Slitting the point you want to bend will enable you to shape the branch properly.

Keeping your elbows close to your body, apply pressure with your thumbs to the spot you want to bend. If the material is a fleshy grass-like plant, crush it slightly beforehand at the desired bend. Crushing will not damage the tough, water-transporting fibers of even the most delicate plants.

Fig. 5. Bending a stalk with the fingertips.

WEDGING AND BENDING

In branches too tough even for the slit method, make a cut from the outside with a saw. The depth should vary with the texture of the wood, but in most cases a cut about two-thirds the thickness of the branch will suffice. After making the cut, find another branch of about the same thickness as the one you are working with, and using your saw, cut from it a V-shaped wedge thick enough to achieve the desired bend and deep enough to fill the slit in the first branch.

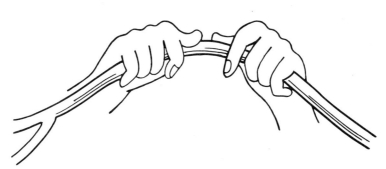

Fig. 6. Holding a thick stalk in front of the body to bend it.

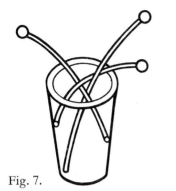

Fig. 7.

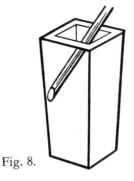

Fig. 8.

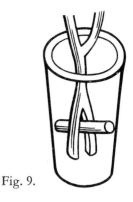

Fig. 9.

7. FIXING MATERIALS IN VASES

SLIT THE STALK

In most of the deeper jar- and bottle-shaped vases, to keep your flowers where you want them, cut small pieces of branch in lengths that will fit firmly either straight or diagonally across the inside of the vase. Cut slits in the bottoms of the stems of the floral materials and fit them on the braces in the vase. The drawings give you ideas of some ways to do this (Figs. 9, 10, 11).

Fig. 10.

NO BRACES AT ALL

Place one stalk firmly in the vase, and prop all the other flowers against it (Fig. 7).

SINGLE-FLOWER PROP

Fix a single flower in place by propping it against the side of a vase as shown in the illustration (Fig. 8).

FORK PROP

Cut a short stalk, cut a slit in the bottom of the material, fit the two together, and put them into the vase (Figs. 12, 13).

Fig. 11.

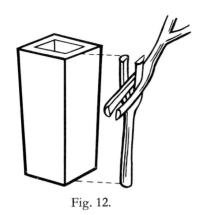

Fig. 12.

Fig. 13.

CROSS BRACE

For wider spacing among the flowers, make a cross brace by tying small bits of stalk together, slip the cross into the vase, and arrange the materials around it (Fig. 14).

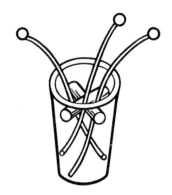

Fig. 14.

WIRE HOLDER

If the shape of the vase makes kenzan or stick braces either unsightly or impractical, ball up some fine wire, put it in the bottom of the vase, and fix the materials in it (Fig. 15).

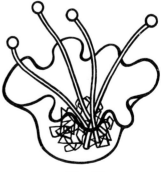

Fig. 15.

8. THE KENZAN

The kenzan, a flower holder made of many small nails set in a heavy base, is highly important because not only does it hold the flowers in place, it also acts as a counterweight to prevent them from falling over. The placement of the kenzan in the vase is very important. In flat, tray-like, shallow vases the flowers themselves seem to alter their appearance depending on the position of the kenzan. Although kenzan come in any number of shapes, let us take a rectangular one as an example and consider different ways of placing it. In flat tray-like vases, except for special effects, avoid the center, and put the kenzan in one corner because putting it in the center, by making the arrangement look like a potted plant, deprives it of the special ikebana flare. Using either the front left or right or the rear left or right corners brings the vase itself to life and makes it possible to effectively use much more of its area. You need not, however, fill the entire vase with flowers simply because the space is available. Instead, put flowers in only a part, and work out an arrangement of spatial balance with the remainder. After all, a gardener does not pack his entire garden with flowers just because he has plenty of space. Placing the kenzan in the corners of the vase makes possible more spacious and better use of the vase and enlivens the spaces, produces a sense of dimensionality in the arrangement, and makes a unity of vase and flowers. With its short side parallel to the front of the vase a rectangular kenzan can better support the weight of the plants.

When using kenzan made of interlocking circles, put the complete circle in the front and the crescent in the back. Place flowers in the front half of the kenzan first and gradually move to the rear because this makes it easier to hide the kenzan itself. On the other hand, start at the rear of the kenzan when you are using large branches in slanting positions. Fill the circle first and then the crescent. Fix heavy branches on the complete circle part of the kenzan, not on the crescent. For thick branches that must lean either to the left or to the right, face the short end of a rectangular kenzan in the direction of the desired lean.

To prevent a kenzan from sliding on the bottom of the vase, slip a piece of paper, cut the same size, under it.

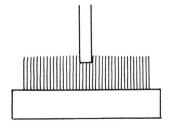 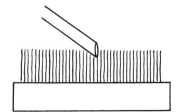

Fig. 16.

Kenzan With Various Materials

1. Slender Materials

A. Chrysanthemums and dahlias.

Cut the stems straight across, and thrust them on the needles from straight above so that the bottoms of the stalks reach the bases of the needles.

B. Flowers with branches as thick as a pencil.

Since these stalks are cut at an angle, thrust them firmly between the needles.

C. Such flowers as pinks and Chinese bellflowers.

Flowers whose stalks are too slender to fit on the needles or to stand up if inserted among them should be wrapped in paper for about one or two centimeters at the bottoms of their stalks and then inserted among the needles.

D. Wild lilies, carnations, etc.

To materials whose blossoms are heavy enough to bend their stalks, add a larger supplementary base, about six or eight centimeters long, and insert this among the kenzan needles.

A few, but naturally not all, of the ways to place the kenzan.

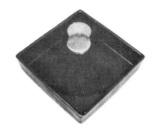

E. Amaryllis and dahlias
When using large, hollow stems, first select another stem small enough to fit into the hollow; then fix this core stem on the kenzan at the desired angle. Slip the real material over it.

Insert a core stalk for fragile hollow stems before fixing them on the kenzan spikes.

2. *Woody materials*

Because most woody materials are too hard to fix on the kenzan, cut a few slits in the bases of the stalks with scissors. With slender branches, simply cutting the bottom on an angle should be enough, but the cut itself must face upward when the material is at the desired slant. It is sometimes difficult to make the slits you need in very thick materials, and even if you do succeed in making them, the material is often too hard to set properly. In such cases, cut away from one half to two thirds of the area of the bottom and make your slits in the remainder.

(left) A slender stem inserted into a larger one set on the kenzan spikes; (right) stem wrapped in cotton before being set on the kenzan.

9. PRESERVATION METHODS

Cutting Under Water

Fill a bucket or a deep bowl with fresh water, and after inserting, the stems of your materials into the water, cut them. Cut the materials two or three times, removing about three centimeters of the stalk each time. Leave the materials in the water for about ten minutes after cutting because the water pressure helps promote evaporation from the leaves and a resulting water intake. Use this same method on flowers just cut from the garden.

Charring

Quickly char the cut ends of floral materials over a gas flame, alcohol lamp, or candle. Wrap the flowers themselves in paper to protect them from the heat, but char the cut ends of the stalks black. Dip them in cold water immediately. Carbonizing the stem ends both stimulates the plant and prevents bacteria growth (Fig. 17).

Hot-water Teatment

Wrap the blossoms and the upper parts of the material in paper, and dip the cut ends in hot water. This is an effective method for tender, soft materials (Fig. 18).

Upside-Down Treatment

Hold flowers cut in the fields upside down, dip them in cold water, wrap them in newspaper, moisten the paper, and lay the flowers on their sides for about thirty minutes.

For long lasting flowers keep them in cool places out of strong, direct sunlight or wind. Change the water often, and keep it cool. In hot weather, it is effective to add a little ice.

Cutting And Crushing

Making horizontal and vertical cuts in the ends of materials or crushing the ends with scissors will improve their ability to take in water.

Fig. 17.   Charring the cut ends in an alcohol-lamp flame.

Fig. 18.

FLOWERS DIRECT FROM THE GARDEN

Try always to cut flowers from your garden either early in the morning or after the sun is down. Fill a container with water, and take it with you so that you can immediately cut your flowers under water and let them stand for a good drink. Be sure you do this with such flowers as morning glories and hydrangeas. Sprinkle a pinch of salt around camelia stamens, and spray the blossom with a fine mist. The salt will cause the pollen to rise and prevent the blossom from shedding its petals. Should a particulalry lovely camelia blossom drop, carefully fix the petals in place again with a toothpick (Fig. 19).

ATOMIZER

Spraying arrangements with an atomizer keeps them fresh looking, particularly in the summer, but take great care to spray only the leaves and *not* the flowers (Fig. 20).

Fig. 19.

Figs. 20.

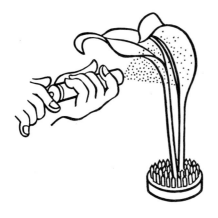

SALT

In almost all cases, and particulaily in those of African daisies and Chinese bellflowers, rubbing salt, baking soda, or alum into the cut ends causes the structure of the plant to contract and increases the area open for water intake.

THICK BAMBOO

For bamboo five or six centimeters in diameter, the following method is effective.

1. Trim the leaves as you want them, and let the bamboo stand in deep water.
2. Insert an iron rod into the bamboo to break the separating walls, but leave the top partition intact.
3. Pour hot salted water into the stalk till it rises to the level of the cut end. The salt solution should be about one teaspoon of salt to one cup of water.
4. Make a plug with a wad of cloth

to keep the water from leaking out when you arrange the bamboo. Replace the salt water as it evaporates and be sure that you put your cloth stopper deep enough into the stalk to hide it. Treated this way, even fairly large pieces of bamboo will last for a long time.

Wild Flowers

Either take a container of water with you when you go gathering wild flowers; or moisten some cotton, cloth, or tissue paper thoroughly, wrap the stems of the plants in it, and secure them with string or a rubber band; or put the root ends in a plastic bag, secure it with a rubber band, wrap the entire plant with newspaper, tie both ends to keep out the wind, and carry the package with the blossoms downward. Do not touch the flowers or in any way transfer your body heat to them.

Chemical Treatment

Certain chemicals lenghten the lives of cut flowers. After cutting materials with the underwater method, let them stand for from ten to twenty minutes in weak solutions of water and alcohol, ascetic acid, peppermint oil, or tincture of capsicum. The solution must be weak, for the chemicals can cause the leaves to shrivel and discolor. A few drops of apple vinegar added to the water in the vase will do wonders for pampas grasses, millet, and other grains and grassy plants. Alcohol and the acids are good for wisteria. A little alum added to the water in the vase is a good preservative.

Injection Pump

To give lotuses, water lilies, and nuphar the extra water they require, use an injection pump. Prepare a solution of tobacco water by wrapping cigarette ends in cloth and soaking them in water, or boil some tea till it is quite strong. Using your injection pump, fill the stalks of both the leaves and the blossoms with one of these solutions, and seal the cut end with alum. This is an effective way to make fresh and healthy materials last longer (Fig. 21).

Figs. 21. Pumping water into stems with a syphon.

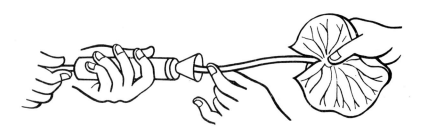

Chapter Two
Floral Folio

The following arrangements should help you evolve notions of ikebana. Do not slavishly copy what I have done. I suggest, on the other hand, that you might find it useful to attempt to duplicate some of my arrangements to cultivate your sense of balance and color judgement. When you have done a number of reproductions of this sort, express your own ideas, emotions, and aspirations through the never-ending fascination of flowers.

I begin my series with a few minimum arrangements, which use a very small number of flowers and leaves to create a mood. Following this with some comments on floral arrangements for special purposes, such as fashion shows or exhibitions, I move on to floral arrangements for festive occasions, and close the folio with my floral impressions of some of the countries, cities, and famous places I visited during my trips around the world on the business of ikebana.

My readers will, by now, have noticed that my approach to ikebana is both creative and feminine. Since I am a woman, this is only natural, but my emphasis on the female in the art of flower arrangement has another source as well. Although many of the great theoreticians of ikebana have been men, I feel that the future of the art lies in the hands of the ladies for two reasons.

Firstly, women have long been intimately associated with flowers. Called by such names as Lily, Rose, and sometimes Daisy, they are even more often given floral attributes by their sweethearts and husbands. "O my Luve's like a red, red rose," is only one of thousands of poetic turns comparing the lady of the piece to flowers. I suspect that in your attic, in a bundle of letters bound with ribbons, you will find lines that, though perhaps less than Shakespearean, mean much to you because in them someone dear says your hands are "white as lilies" or your eyes are "dewy violets."

Mere associations and poetic metaphors, however, are insufficient cause to grant charge of the future of ikebana to the female sex. Much stronger reason is to be found in woman's psychological approach to flowers and their arrangement.

Great Japanese male flower arrangers have set patterns and created schools that now dominate the entire field. According to precepts established by these masters, the blossoms themselves are subservient to a traditionally established code in which orthodoxy is not only safe, but also satisfying.

Regarding flowers as living things with rich and varied artistic possibilities, women find the rules and schools devised by men restricting. They long to express what is in their hearts by letting the flowers speak freely for them, but because as does any other art, ikebana requires a degree of basic technical skill, guidance is essential.

Convinced that women are best suited to carry on the living creativity of ikebana and aware of the importance of aesthetic education in the cultivation of skill in art, I have evolved a new approach to floral arrangement—creative ikebana.

Why do I feel it important to divorce myself from established schools, and what is the distinguishing element in creative ikebana that justifies its existence? I think what I have said about the female longing for free expression in flowers and the sterility of copying orthodox patterns clearly outlines the need for a new departure, but it does not answer the second part of my rhetorical question.

When one breaks away from established patterns and attempts expression on one's own, an image is the first essential. Without some idea of a destination, progress is impossible. The presence of an image, an idea, emotion, or atmosphere to be expressed in floral terms, is the element that sets creative ikebana apart from the schools. Whereas, in orthodox arrangements, the flower must serve the needs of traditional rules, in creative ikebana, the image alone governs the selection lengths, colors, and placement of materials.

Although the traditional approach always insures balanced arrangements, balance alone is not of paramount importance. Creativity brings greater satisfaction to the human soul than any other activity, and knowing when and how to destroy balance for the sake of aesthetic effect is an essential element in the creative process. It is the ability to distinguish between the aesthetically satisfying and the trivial, between the stimulating and the stultifying, that I want to develop in the students of creative ikebana because I want them to know the joys of producing works of beauty.

The joys of creation are of two sorts: the pure and the adulterated. In its pure form, springing from the act of making something that did not exist in an identical form, this joy is unlike any other feeling mankind knows. In its adulterated—its more frequent—form it is related to the purposes the created things must serve. Among the noblest of the functions creativity can fill is giving happiness, to one's self, of course, but even greater, to others.

Creative ikebana can fill these roles by letting you enjoy again—this time in flowers—memories, scenes, even people you once knew. The images of past things in your heart is waiting to be expressed aesthetically in flowers.

Giving happiness to others is simple with flowers. Think how happy the invalid is to receive a floral piece you arranged yourself or how much happier a birthday is if you enhance it with your own floral interpretation of the day or of the person celebrating it.

1. MINIMUM ARRANGEMENTS

Throughout the history of Japanese floral art run two opposed tastes, both existing side by side as early as the Momoyama period (1568-1615). One finds its most perfect expression in the elaborate and gorgeous *rikka* style of arrangement; the other is best exemplified in the simple single-blossom, single-leaf arrangements suited to the refined and rustic tastes of the tea ceremony. By selecting one or perhaps two blossoms and combining them with a few leaves we are able to emphasize both color, the keynote of Occidental art, and form, the element dearest to the Japanese heart.

Defining in words the simple style of beauty that became a Japanese aesthetic characteristic after the middle ages is difficult. Briefly, however, I feel that it sprang from the ideas of that same Zen Buddhism which has become an important element in the spiritual activity of the whole world. I assert this because the *nageire* style of arrangement, which uses few flowers, arose to meet the needs of the tea ceremony, in itself an outgrowth of Zen tea-drinking practices. Doubtless, the people who were developing ikebana fell under the influence of the tea ceremony and, through it, of Zen. Although this reason may seem superficial, I think no one can deny the extremely Zen-like feeling of the single-blossom, single-leaf style of arranging.

The aim of seated Zen meditiation is to clear away all spiritual hindrances and to unify the human heart. A basic tenet of Zen says that one contains all. I feel that to the degree that one flower manifests the whole universe, the same aim applies to the single-blossom, single-leaf style of ikebana. Is this approach too mystical for the Occidental mind? Perhaps it seems mere intuition; it certainly will not fit the mold of rationality. But the fact is that Western philosphers have already built too rational a house. They have reasoned and ordered things so well that they now totally lack the all-important "one" that contains all. Consequently, the people following such philosophies lead lives of spiritual disorder and confusion.

Do not think that I am attempting to attribute the ikebana aesthetic of a single blossom and a single leaf solely to Zen Buddhism; I merely indicate the existence in floral art of an idea similar to one that dominates this famous discipline.

Another concept similar to the idea that flower arrangements are more meaningful made from fewer materials can be found in the now famous Japanese haiku, a seventeen-syllable poetic form the content of which is pared to a minimum but the associative meaning of which can be limitless.

At this point, please let me assure you that reducing the number of flowers and leaves does not necessarly mean that arranging them is an easy task. On the contrary, suggesting the entire universe in one flower and one leaf demands the most devoted effort. I should warn you that taking "simplication" and "reduction to a minimum" too literally, invites the danger of producing geometrical and cold arrangements. In single-blossom, single-leaf arrangements you must strive for purity and eliminate rigidity.

Examining a flower, you find unity, but in the slight distortions in the stalk, or in texture, and in the individuality of each petal you also see the infinite element of chance inherent in all nature. At its most profound, the single-blossom, single-leaf style of arranging strives to place the flowers so that in their simplicity they suggest the infinite variety of the world of nature.

The Japanese fondness for balance achieved without geometrical symmetry further creates a sense of the universal in the particular. German architect and critic, Bruno Taut, noted this trait in his comments on the exquisite placement of the gardens and buildings at the Katsura Detached Palace. The same regard for chance results occurs in Japanese ceramics where irregular color patterns and surfaces are highly prized. Indeed, in almost all phases of Japanese art, the natural, the non-geometrical, and the asymmetrical are important.

Though all of this applies to the single-blossom, single-leaf style of arrangement, I do not claim that this is the entire meaning of ikebana. I simply say that ikebana recognizes this aesthetic principle and that, as in the haiku, it often attempts to show the larger world in small floral terms. Furthermore, I feel that a consciousness of what I might call "abbreviated beauty" helps to develop your own creative flower interpretations of the natural environment around you.

The apparently simple things are not necessarily the easiest, but they are often the most spiritually satisfying. Look through the arrangements on the next few pages. Try some of them; then work out your own minimum arrangements.

Materials: dahlias and loquat leaf
Container: black, double-mouth vase from Romania
Here is a study in varying forms and colors: the free-form, black vase, the brown oval of the dried loquat leaf, and the vibrant gold circles of the dahlia blooms. The harmony between the vase and the materials is very important.
Note: Dry the loquat leaves in the shade to make them last, longer.

Materials: dried grass and one poppy bud

Container: vase from Sweden

A single glowing poppy bud combined with long plumes of golden grass. Uncomplicated and relaxing, yet charged with profound pleasure and beauty.

Materials: woodrose and wild grapes
Containers: handmade ceramic vases
Two small vases, as well wedded as a happy couple, and a limited number of flowers and leaves compose a touching piece, which is also a profound source of joy.

Materials: monkshood and palm nuts
Container: ceramic vase
A simple arrangement brings a touch of mystic beauty into the home and becomes a source of pleasure for arranger and viewer alike. The palm nuts look like fireworks, but the monkshood is the protagonist of the piece.

Materials: artichoke blossoms and a rubber-tree leaf
Container: glass vase
Two serene artichoke blossoms set in motion by a shooting diagonal rubber-tree leaf, an arrangement that is completely at home in any room.

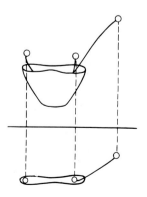

Materials: one fatsia leaf; Japanese pampas
Container: base of an Italian lamp
This simple arrangement, a floral song of heartfelt
welcome, is easy to make on the spur of the moment when unexpected guests arrive. The green
of the fatsia leaf reflects the yellow line of the
container, which, an article of daily use instead
of an orthodox vase, adds a touch of new
interest.

2. IMAGE ARRANGEMENTS

An image is the first essential of creative ikebana. Select anything you like, an emotion, a scene, a friend, a song, a poem;
and imagine ways to capture in flowers the heart of that image.
Through your own highly personal, subjective representation,
if you have a good eye and a sincere approach to your materials, your image will communicate to others. All flower
arrangements begin and end with an image. On the following
few pages you will find some that I have tried. Look at them
carefully; then try your own.

FANTASY I

Materials: orchids, dried ferns, and mountain ferns
Container: hanging vase

The passionate cerise orchids and the bleached white ferns take
on an aura of fantasy and mystery as they turn slowly in the
breeze.

FUNNY FACES

Materials: latifolia and fox faces

Container: black boat-shaped vase from Switzerland.

I have used the already humorous fox faces, a cousin of the eggplant, together with a big spray of latifolia to give a feeling of bubbling gaiety.

FANTASY II

Materials: Japanese quince
Container: gray glass vase
To evoke a feeling of fancy, I emphasized the natural quality of the quince and let it envelope the vase in sharp accented lines. The real beauty of this new kind of arrangement springs from the individual quality of the plant. Use all your flowers so as to underscore their special features.

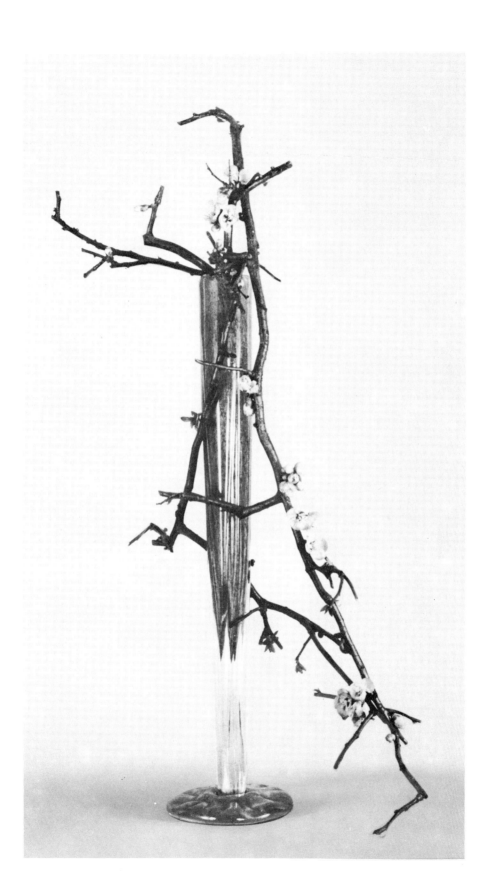

PASSION

Materials: tulips, eucalyptus, and milioglastus
Container: glass vase with red stripes
I have cut the tulip petals to suggest the special passion a
great actor has during a performance. The reds of the vase
and of the tulips are fiery and impressive. Milioglastus, a lovely
year-round green, breaks easily; be careful with it.

INTELLECT

Materials: rose and coral
Container: slender bottle from Holland
A single pink rose against a lacy fan of coral represents clarity
and intellect.

NORTH WIND

Materials: dried sunflower and Chinese quince
Container: black and white striped vase
Wrapped in a hood and braving the cold the
round-faced children never stop running.
The humorous quince and the dried sunflower combine in a strikingly appealing
fairytale way.

LOVE

Materials: roses and palm
Container: Chinese bronze vase
The two roses glow like love eternal in the
lasting grace of the dried palm.

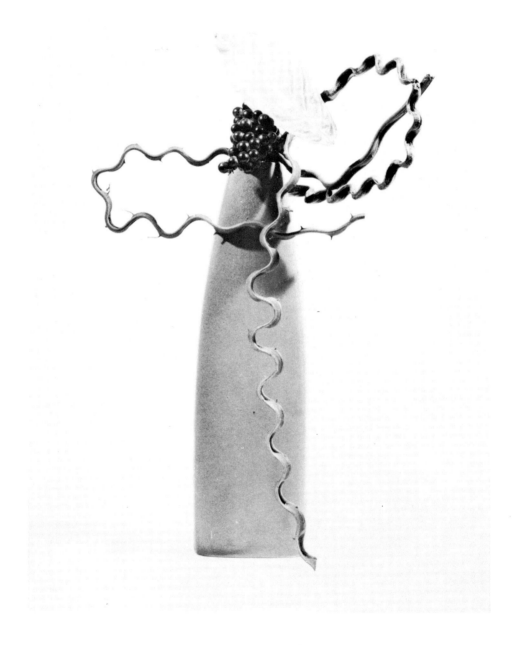

A Tale Of The Fruitful Fall

Materials: mulberry and grapes
Container: slender, dark brown vase
The beautiful color and form of the grapes combined with
the dried leaf and the swirling movement of the mulberry
branches produce a balanced composition containing both
movement and calm. Use available fruits and leaves such
as chestnuts, persimmons, tangerines, quince, or pomegranates
on the bough, as well as bright autumn leaves, chrysanthemums, or Chinese quince to give the feeling of autumn.

Autumnal Calm

Materials: castor, black vine, dried lotus pods
Container: black pottery vase
The effective contrasts of the red and pink of the maple-
shaped castor leaves and black of the materials and the vase
remind one of the other paintings of the so-called Southern
School of Chinese artists or of a fanciful autumnal atmosphere.

Happy Heart

Materials: bleached hemp palm, red gladiolus, and berries
Container: glass vase
Berries dancing for joy inside the transparent vase and swirls of white hemp palm focus attention on the cluster of bright red gladiolus, the smiling heart of the composition.

ANTICIPATING AUTUMN

Materials: bleached hemp palm leaves, chestnuts
in husk, Turkish bellflowers
Container: smoky, green glass vase
In late August, I start wanting to arrange such
autumnal materials as chestnuts. The bleached
hemp palm leaves thrust into the mouth of the
bottle hold the chestnuts in place and provide
movement to right and left.

Above the leafless chestnuts rise delicately
tinted lavender Turkish bellflowers. Flowers can
help us hurry the seasons along faster.

ELEGANCE

Materials: carnations, erica, sweet peas, and pussy willow
Container: French glass vase
The carnations are elegant, and the pussy willow is youthful. The erica and the sweet peas round out the shape of the whole and add a note of refinement and repose.

3. FLORAL GRAND TOUR

Permit me to show you my impressions of some of the places
I have visited in my trips around the world. In no case have I
attempted to give concrete representation to scenes or things.

These are my memories; I hope they will communicate to you
and inspire you to create for yourself.

SYMBOLIC FLOWERS OF CZECHOSLOVAKIA

In all my yearly travels to Europe I have rarely
found a country more charming than Czechoslovakia, the home of glittering Bohemian glass.
Beside the Bridge of Carl IV, from which one
can enjoy a view of the Gothic cathedrals and
a Renaissance castle, are stone pavements and
mosaic pedestrian walks, and along it at night gas
lamps illuminate Prague, "the jewel in the crown
of Europe," as Goethe called it. I have combined
the beauty of the old bridge with the glowing
yellow of golden rain, a flower loved by Goethe
and redolent of the hues of this country.

CHRISTI
CRUCI
FIXI
CONSTRI
CTA
BRACHIO

SANCTA
LUTGAR
DIS
ORDINIS
CISTERCI
ENSIS

GERMANY

Materials: lotus and yellow roses.
Container: vase from Bonn
With these yellow roses I have tried to suggest
a castle I saw gleaming gold in the light of the
dying sun high above the Rhine.

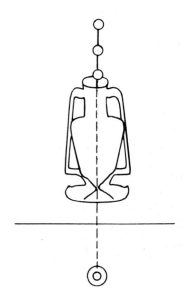

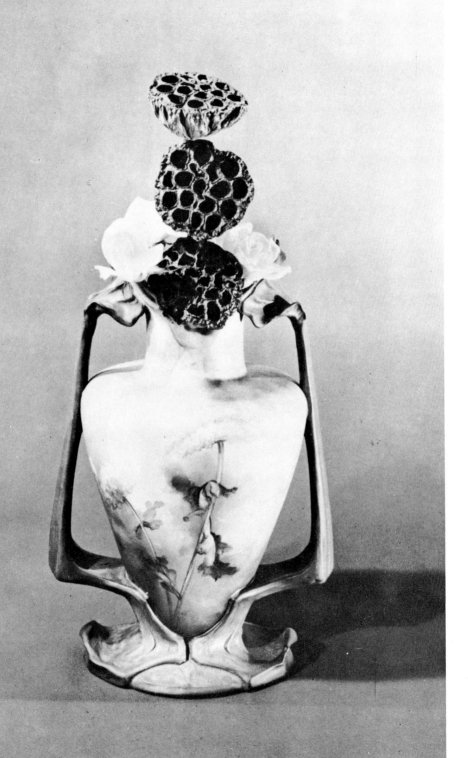

LIMA, PERU

Materials: dried materials, Japanese pampas grass, ananas
Container: pot of Inca design
The charm of the Inca pot combined with dried floral materials whispers of ages long dead, tales of the glory of the Inca and of the streets of Lima, shrouded in gray mists.

LOS ANGELES

Materials: rape seed, wheat, carnations, and milioglastus
Container: glass vase designed by the author.
This mixture of seeds and bright sunny flowers breathes the
open air of California and the City of the Angels.
Note: Carnations, native to Southern Europe, are lovely used
singly or in masses acentuating the color, rather than the form,
of the fragrant blossoms.

TAIWAN

Materials: herbaceous peony
Container: bud vase
A single white herbaceous peony recalls my first visit to exotic Taiwan
Note: Almost as famous as its showy cousin, the tree peony, the herbaceous peony blooms in May and June. A single flower—they come in red, white, purple, and striped varieties—floating in a flat dish is lovely.

BRAZIL ▶

Materials: dried materials from Brazil, ananas
Container: vase designed by the author
Colorful, showy ananas and dried materials attempt to recall the rythmical movement that flows through the streets of Rio de Janiero and São Paulo.

Throughout Central and South America ananas, first cousin of the pineapple, grow in abundance.

SWITZERLAND

Materials: calla and yellow glass marbles
Container: crystal vase.
The arrangement suggests the sound of the waters
of Alpine lakes.
Note: Do not use calla leaves because their water
intake is poor.

SYMBOLIC FLOWERS OF HOLLAND

Materials: double tulips and onion.
Container: a black Dutch vase

Using a note of loveliness like that created by a mother carrying a child, I have attempted to symbolize the riotous cavalcade of tulip blooms for which the Netherlands are famous.

ITALY ▶

Materials: orchids, New Zealand flax, and bleached mountain fern
Container: majolica vase
The combination of the New Zealand flax, the luxurious orchids, and the traditional vase reminds one of the romance of Italy.
Note: New Zealand flax is very straight and rigid used as it is. For a more romantic effect bend it to make the spaces of the arrangement seem larger. Burry the orchids in a bed of bleached fern.

MEMORY OF MEXICO

Materials: dried leaves and cosmos blossoms
Contatiner: Mexican basket
Both the sunny casual beauty of the flowers and the basket,
which I bought from some natives in Mexico, bring back the
warmth and friendliness of that country.
Note: Cosmos have good water intake. If you merely cut them
under water, they should last a long while.

HAWAII

Materials: bleached hemp palm, kaffir lily, bird of paradise
Container: hat from Hawaii

Beautifully bleached hemp palm leaves highlight a cluster of
kaffir lily and bird of paradise blossom. The hat, woven and
sold on the beach at Waikiki, suggests rolling surf and flying
spray.

SPANISH DANCE

Materials: holly (*Ilex serrata*)
Container: Spanish glass bottle
The swirling holly beautifully unites in color and form with the bottle to suggest the passion, brilliance, and dazzling action of a flamenco dancer.

NORTHERN EUROPE

Materials: dried materials
Container: Danish vase
An expression of the clarity and cleanliness of the
Scandinavian air.
Note: Carefully balance the and forms.

Symbolic Flowers Of Poland

The vicinity of the Chopin residence at Zelazowa Wola, fifty kilometers west of Warsaw, is now a public park. Among the cool green trees of what was once a part of the home of the Count Skarbek, I tried to represent in spiraea (*Spiraea cantonensis*) lavendar and white lilacs, and bleached mountain fern an evocation of the music of this great composer—as I heard it played in his house— and to contrast the artificiality of the music with the singing of the birds and the rustling of the leaves. My heart was filled with gladness because I was able to visit the home of my favorite composer.

SYMBOLIC FLOWERS OF HUNGARY

Damson branches with green leaves and a few bright red roses in a folk-craft, white vase ornamented with blue and set in a corner of the old Fisherman's Fort overlooking Budapest and the Danube recall the true flavor of Hungary.

4. FLOWERS AND PEOPLE

In my trips around the world, I came up with
the idea of representing in floral terms the impressions and images made upon me by some of
the famous people I met. Marcel Marceau, Marc
Chagall, and the others pictured here are just a
few of the celebreties I have tried to symbolize
in flowers. When my choice of flowers coincides
with the person's favorite blossoms, I am very
happy indeed.

(With the courtesy of the Chuokoron-sha.)

TWIGGY

When I visited their studio in London, Twiggy's manager, Justin de Villeneuve, graciously opened the door for me, and in a few moments, rippling the air around her like a swallow, Twiggy herself appeared. Shyly biting her nails, she offered me a cup of tea. Four of her boyfriends, including Justin, constantly surrounded her with bright laughter.

Noticing a large orange straw hat hanging on the wall, I said—to Twiggy's great surprise—that I should like to use it as a vase. With baby's breath and purple asters I tried to capture this charming model's clean loveliness. Her four friends applauded as we photographed her sitting in a chair with the hat and flowers in her lap.

93

DALIDA

All Parisians agree that their city's top chanteuse is the phoenix of song, Dalida. With two rich stalks of pink gladiolus I attempted to capture the thrilling beauty of this singer as, with tears in her eyes and trembling hands, she sang of passionate love and broken hearts.

(With the courtesy of the Chuokoron-sha.)

(With the courtesy of the Chuokoron-sha.)

FAIRYLAND PRINCE AND PRINCESS

Lichtenstein, a country of under 20,000 people, nestles high in the Alps. Its Crown Prince and his lovely Princess live in a fairyland chateau beside a beautiful lake. To represent the royal pair and their romance I selected snowy white lilies, and to suggest their devoted subjects I used a few glowing talisman roses.

MADEMOISELLE

Materials: bleached white mountain ferns, wisteria vine, violets
Container: pink and white striped French glass decanter
I lifted the stopper of the decanter slightly and slipped the materials in between it and the sides of the bottle. The loop of wisteria vine on the right both keeps the stopper in place and provides a touch of chic. Violets are simple yet charged with emotional appeal. They are extremely pleasing bunched lightly together.

WOMAN OF THE NILE

Materials: southern pine cones and African daisies
Container: ceramic container from Cairo
I have attempted to recall the mysterious women
I met in front of the great pyramids during my
visit to Egypt. A sense of the timelessness of one
of the world's oldest civilizations, of the life-
giving flow of the Nile, and of the great monu-
ments of the past underlies the tones and forms
of this piece. The pink and bright red African
daisies suggest the women of this ancient land.

LADY OF BRAZIL

Materials: anthurium, dried white flowers from Brazil
Container: ceramic vase designed by the author
The red anthurium suggests the sensuality of the people of Brazil and the blazing Brazilian sun dropping suddenly behind the evening horizon. It also recalls a lovely Brazilian women standing near one of the nation's many fountains.

5. FESTIVE ARRANGEMENTS

Nothing brightens a birthday, Christmas, Easter, or any other holiday as much as an arrangement of flowers designed with the special flavor of the festival. I have selected a few holidays, some Japanese and some international, and have used the materials and colors traditionally associated with them to suggest ways to highlight holidays with blossoms. Every locality has its own festivals; and every festival, its traditions. Select the materials closely associated with holidays in your land; or better yet, find a new material, and use it in a fresh way to express the feeling of some cherished festival.

RED AND WHITE HANGING NEW-YEAR ARRANGE-
MENT

Materials: pine and *Chloranthus glaber,* red and
white *mizuhiki* (a ceremonial ornament made of
wires)
Container: hanging bamboo vase designed by the
author
The *mizuhiki*, a traditional ornament with a
number of ceremonial uses, gives this modern
New-Year arrangement just the right festive
touch. Old-fashioned greens preserve a traditional feeling.

BIRTHDAY FLOWERS

Materials: red ginger flowers, bleached mulberry, and dried snake gourds
Container: tall white vase from Romania

Although in times gone by, we Japanese arranged only pine or crysanthemum for festive occassions, today, as our environment has changed, so have our tastes in arrangements. Now, instead, of large floral groups, lighter, more imaginative ones are in vogue. In a tall white Romanian vase, twisting, wiry bleached mulberry, glowing, dried snake gourds, and flaming ginger, combine for a keynote of freshness and airy grace. For happy birthday flowers, include candles or ribbons; anything will be fine, as long as you plan your arrangement to emphasize the beauty of materials and the desired mood. Incidentally, red and white, the tonal highlights of this arrangement, are the colors we Japanese use on most auspicious occasions.

GREETING THE NEW YEAR

Materials: pine with moss, white camelia, kumquats, gold and silver *mizuhiki* ornament.

Container: long, low, gold-colored vase

The undying green beauty of the pine, particularly of those coated with silvery moss, is a favorite Japanese trim for the New Year. I have combined its sturdy dignity with the umblemished loveliness of a white camelia and with the rosy-gold of a few kumquats. To highlight the horizontality of the total plan and to intensify the Japanese-holiday feeling, I have added a *mizuhiki* ornament made of gold and silver, paper-covered wires.

Clean the camelia leaves thoroughly, and shake a little salt into the center of the blossom so that the petals will last longer.

All the materials for this arrangement should be specially fresh and clean because they must symbolize the beginning of a new year.

NEW-YEAR FANCY ▶

Materials: pine and red nandin berries
Container: hourglass-shaped vase
Red berries rise from the depths of the vase like the morning sun out of the sea on the first day of the year. The strong, rich branch of fragrant pines soars upward, a symbol of hope for the new year.

Dolls' Day

Materials: sweet peas and peach blossoms
Container: double-mouth black vase
To suggest a mood proper to Dolls' Day, or the Girls' Day Festival, March 3, a distinctive and gentle Japanese holiday, I have used feminine and traditional, soft pink peach blossoms and bright, gay, lemon colored sweet peas. Using only a few flowers emphasizes the loveliness of little girls and suggests the first buds of early spring. The bold lines of the peach branches add vitality. Fit the cut end of the branch securely against the inside of the vase. Versatile peach blossoms go beautifully with roses, tulips, acacia, and many other colorful flowers.

BOY'S DAY

Materials: iris and rushes
Container: Italian ceramic vase
Iris, the proud strong symbol of the male, always
ornament Japanese homes on Boy's Day, the
fifth of May. Straight, forceful lines and strong,
virile flowers evoke both the atmosphere of the
ponds where the iris grow and the masculine
mood of the festival.

Carefully select flowers to combine with
iris: spiraea creates a nice blend of line movement, and summer chrysanthemums complement
them pleasantly.

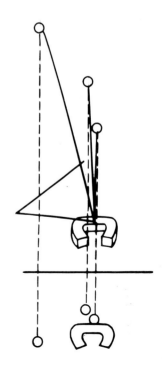

6. POESY OF
BLOSSOMS

In this group I have attempted to evoke a mood, the general taste and smell of a time of the year, a kind of weather, or a festival feeling. Naturally, all my moods are basically Japanese; you must select materials and vases to create those indicative of both your personality and surroundings. The success of the arrangement will depend on the harmony between materials and vase.

FLORAL PATTERN

Materials: wild rose seed pods, monstera leaves, and white lilies
Container: folk-craft ceramic vase
The long, resiliant branches of wild rose spreading horizontally suggest a fine-line drawing of a summer- flower

pattern, whereas the four or five restful green monstera leaves provide both strength and volume. White lilies, all cut to the same length, are grouped at the side of the mouth of the vase. Instead of white lilies, try roses, sunflowers, or dahlias. Cutting them all to the same height empha-sizes the strong summer floral colors and heightens the beauty of the tonal scheme.

Note: Simply cutting under water should permit adequate water intake for all three materials, but submerging the monstera leaves for a few minutes will enhance their effect.

PASSION

Materials: flame flowers, bleached wisteria vines, black vines (natural color)
Container: free-form vase with pedestal
The heavy, bold lines of the flaming red flowers (bulbs from Africa) contrast sharply with the staccato movement of the black vines and the sharp clarity of the looping white wisteria. The red and black set each other off well, and the creamy white of the wisteria highlights the whole. When striving for a dramatic arrangement, understand your theme completely, and arrange the flowers to that they speak for themselves.

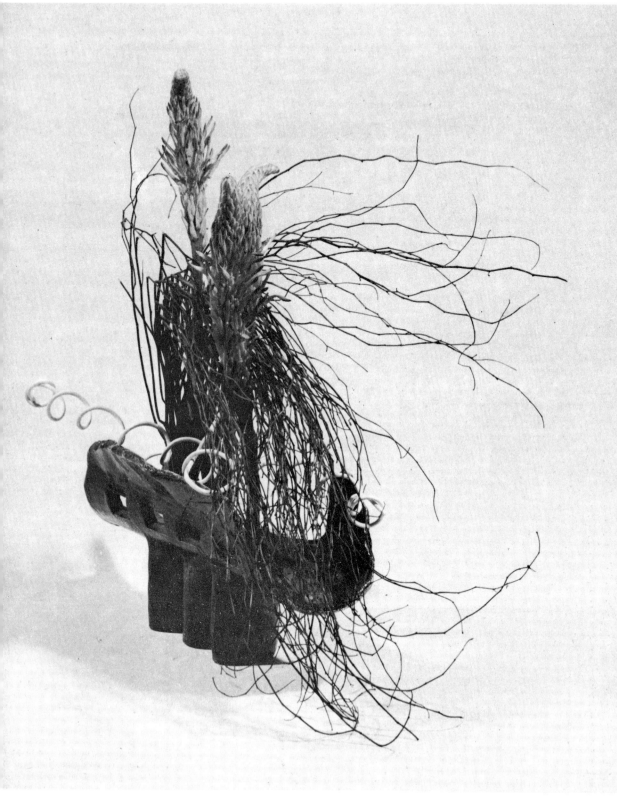

Happy Family

Materials: spiraea, kaffir lily, and small bamboo canes.
Container: modern ceramic vase
The emotion here is warmth and family love. The slender bamboo canes give movement, and the simply treated, gorgeous kafir lily provides a flaming heart for the whole mass. Around them the small white blooms of the spiraea swirl as flakes of light swarming around a happy family.

POEM IN BLOOMS

Materials: berries, pink field clover, and white calla lilies
Container: white ceramic vase
At the heart of the arrangement lies a cluster of creamy callas. Just below them gleam shiny black berries, and on either side flash long arching sprays of pale pink, dried field clover. All of them breathe the air of autumn.

NEATNESS

Materials: aspidistra and calla lily.

Container: Italian glass vase

The straight lines of the calla lily and the grace of the aspidistra harmonize with the fancy curves of the glass vase in a lyrical, yet restrained, composition.

BESIDE THE WATER

Materials: lotus blossoms, caladium leaf, papyrus
Container: white glass pitcher from Finland
Nothing captures the mystic feeling of the edge of a body of
water as well as lotus and papyrus. The sparkling white vase
adds a thrilling note of immaculate beauty. I arranged three
lotus blossoms, but the arrangement somehow grew nicer as
the petals fell from two, leaving only the gold of the pistils
and stamens.

After The Rain

Materials: artichokes, rushes, and caladium leaf
Container: silver-colored ceramic plate

Cool lavender flowers and refreshing white and green leaves against a silver background epitomize the freshness of the first moments after a summer shower. The rushes add accent and suggest the rain that has just passed.

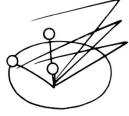

Native to the sides of streams and ponds, rushes set off to great advantage such flowers as iris, nuphar, water lilies, calla lilies, dahlias, and hydrangea. You can develop a wide variety of feelings depending on the way you treat them. They may be bent, woven, plaited, or twisted.

A Song Of Autumn

Materials: Japanese pampas, burnet, *Anthistiria arguens, patrinia scabiosaefolia,* chyrsanthemums, and field clover
Container: bamboo basket

Though autumn is a poetic season filled with the richness of ripe fruits and the splendor of crimson and gold leaves, when seeking materials for an ikebana representation of it, we Japanese almost always turn first to the traditional seven grasses: Japanese pampas (*Miscanthus sinensis*), *patrinia scabio-saefolia,* burnet, Chinese balloon flower, fringed pinks, ague-weed, and arrowroot. I have combined a few of them in a bamboo basket in an attempt to capture the wonderful poetry of autumn. After removing the leaves of the single stalk of pampas grass, I let it tower straight from the side of the basket to represent the bright autumn sky and arranged the pink chyrsanthemums, the yellow *patrinia scabiosaefolia,* the black burnet, and the clover low at the base of the pampas stalk so that their lovely colors are visible through the basket. The *patrinia scabiosaefolia,* one of the earliest blooming of the seven autumn grasses, is often associated with the Bon Festival, held in July or August. Japanese poetry frequently compares its dainty blossoms to the gentle charms of the female sex. Cut short so that only the yellow flowers appear in a mass and set in a modern glass vase, this delicate flower creates quite a different kind of beauty. Cut under water and set for a while in dilute hydrochloric acid, it develops good powers of water absorption.

When using the Japanese pampas grass with the leaves on, spray them with sugar water to help prevent them from dropping.

Evening Breeze

Materials: nuphars and rushes
Container: oblong black ceramic vase
Yellow nuphar blossoms with shiny green leaves, when set short, as if in converse with the water, recall warm summer nights. Arrange the blossoms first, then the leaves. Tall, straight-rising rushes balance the group.
Note: Nuphar blossoms wilt immediately unless you pump the stems full of tobacco solution to promote water intake.

BLIZZARD OF BLOSSOMS

Materials: white spiraea and red tulips
Container: low, rectangular, white ceramic vase
Swirling around a flaming group of red tulips fly
snowflake-like spiraea blossoms. The ability to
create among branches spaces that vitalize an
arrangement is one of the most important ikebana
lessons. I increased the dimensionality of this
arrangement by placing the vase with one corner
forward, thus creating views of the flowers
from three sides. Try replacing the tulips with red
carnations or roses.

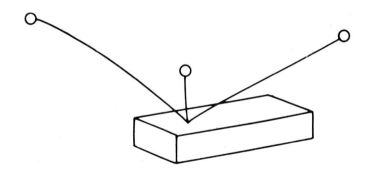

ONCOMING AUTUMN

Materials: oak leaves beginning to change color,
dried branch
Container: vase from Holland
The combination of the softness of the vase and
the brilliance of the oak leaves with the romantic
flavor of the dried branches boldly suggests the
autumn wind. For a softer touch add small crysanthemums, either yellow or white. However,
because their water intake is bad, peel the skin
from the stalk ends, and split them with scissors.
Spray the leaves with sugar water to make them
remain on the branches longer.

ROSE WALZ

Materials: salmon-pink roses, erica, glass balls
Container: two white ceramic compotes, one
inside the other.

Light and sprightly, the branches of pale lavender erica float gracefully out in horizontal lines
from the top compote and from between the
two. In the middle of the top compote I have
put delicate, salmon-pink roses. The crystal balls
placed here and there add a jewel-like gleam.

WINTER FANCY

Materials: Japanese pampas, yellow daffodils, yellow orchids, fox faces

Container: rectangular, black pottery vase

I have placed one kenzan in each end of the vase and have divided the materials into two groups each unified with the other by the swirling pampas. Both the grass and the fox faces are convenient materials for winter when flowers are scarce. The contrasts between the yellows of the daffodils, orchids, and fox faces and the black of the vase are softened to a fanciful winter mood by the silver of the pampas.

THE JOY OF EARLY SPRING ▶

Materials: pine, white orchids, seed pods of the red orchid

Container: footed ceramic vase

Tall, straight, upward-rising pine to symbolize strength, elegant white orchids for purity and beauty, and the seed pods of the red orchid for hope and freshness.

EARLY SUMMER

Materials: wild lilies, baby's breath
Container: hanging glass vase

Heady, fragrant wild lilies and baby's breath,
light and warm as summer mists, rise cloudlike
from the glittering crystal vase. Suspended so
that it moves lightly, the arrangement suggests
summer breezes and balmy poetry-filled midsum-
mer night's dreams.

7. VARIATIONS WITH GLADIOLUS AND DAHLIAS

With only one variety of flower it is possible to create a many different effects. A single flower can become a work of art, or a mass of several blossoms can clearly reveal individuality and special beauty. With your own ideas, you can add a touch of novelty to ordinary blooms. By making the flower and the container a unified whole you can suggest natural vistas. Any number of compact compositions become possible if you carefuly blend the colors and forms of blooms, leaves, and container.

Using Gladiolus I

Materials: red gladiolus and bulrushes
Container: black, half-moon vase

Gladiolus lend themselves to variations, and the naturally straight bulrushes can be bent or twisted into ropes for special effects. This arrangement places small white stones at the bases of rushes, bent into simple angles, and highlights the whole with a single red gladiolus set to express its own individuality.

USING GLADIOLUS II

Materials: two red gladiolus and two stalks of Japanese pampas grass

Container: bamboo basket

Contrary to the preceding arrangement, which expresses the individuality of the gladiolus, this display makes use of their color only. The bright red and the gold of the pampas intensify the effect of the yellow bamboo basket.

Using Dahlias I

Materials: yellow dahlias and palm leaves
Container: Dutch Delft tile watering pot
Dahlias, native to Mexico, come in yellow, white,
red, and purple; their stems are very soft. In this
arrangement, I have placed them against a background of palm leaves and have used the
Delft watering pot as an integral part of the design
to suggest a corner of a flower garden. The dahlias
are set a little high to emphasize the individuality
of the blooms.

Using Dahlias II

Materials: red dahlias and leaves of the *Dendropanax trifidus*

Container: free-form vase

The red of the dahlias—from which I stripped all the leaves—and the greens of the vase and the *Dendropanax trifidus* leaves blend in a harmonious whole.

Cutting under water and applying a little menthol oil to the cut helps the flowers last longer. It is also helpful to remove the leaves.

8. FLOWERS TO BRIGHTEN
DAILY LIVING

Blossom And Lemons In A Tall Glass Vase

Materials: dahlia, two green leaves, and lemons

Container: crystal glass vase

To put the emphasis on the fragrant, lovely yellow lemons in the gleaming, smooth crystal vase, I have used only one flower and two leaves in an arrangement where carefully planning the inside contents of the vase is as important as the placement of the flowers outside. I use no kenzan because I want to preserve the delicate feeling of the glass.

This arrangement would compliment any room in any country.

An Interesting Spatial Composition

Materials: wild grapes, red, white, and pink orchids, and smilax

Container: tall ceramic vase

The smilax and wild grapes develop their own soft, calm space into the middle of which I set the colorful orchids to bring out the pastoral poetry of the composition. This arrangement, particularly suitable for living room tables, is designed to be seen from any direction. (See color illustration on jacket.)

Arrangement That Varies

Materials: caladium leaf and chrys-
mum blossom
Container: sculpture made of *oya* stone
Chrysanthemums or water lilies
floating in dishes set on tables evoke
images of cool refreshing streams,
and this leaf and blossom afloat in
the hollow of a garden sculpture
move and change and always pleases
with their variety.

The water in arrangements of
this kind should be changed frequently because it and the things it reflects
seriously affect the success of the
whole design

LOVELY FROM ANY VANTAGE POINT

Materials: chrysanthemums and dried palm.

Container: pale blue compote

Chrysanthemum blossoms cut short and set low in the elegant, pale compote and combined with the fantastic curves of the palm are striking seen from any point; arrangements like this are suitable for coffee tables or other low places.

STILL-LIFE COMPOSITION

Materials: apple, lemon, dried pomegranate, daisies with roots, melon, ginger, and arrowhead bulbs

Containers: red and black lacquered trays

In combing fruits and vegetables for decorative purposes it is important to advantageously display the colors and forms of the individual items by carefully contrasting the large and the small.

Large leaves (lotus or plantain), trays, dishes, shallow vases, pots, boards, carved dishes, or bamboo are interesting containers for these displays.

ARRANGEMENT WITH A DREAM
Materials: pansies and bleached mulberry vine
Containers: one large and one small triangular vase
Dainty little pansies, innocent as children's faces,
peep from among the spiraling white branches
of bleached mulberry. Lovely, no matter what
the vantage point, this arrangement with a dream
is particularly suitable for children's rooms.

Fragile pansies should be placed quickly with
as little handling as possible.

Chapter Three
Occasional Ikebana

1. ARRANGEMENT'S FOR SPECIAL OCCASIONS

Aside from the important part floral arranging can play in bringing happiness and beauty into our daily life, it can also enliven any number of such occasions as exhibitions, fashion, shows, and conferences. Perhaps the following samples of my work will suggest things for your next neighborhood bazaar or church meeting.

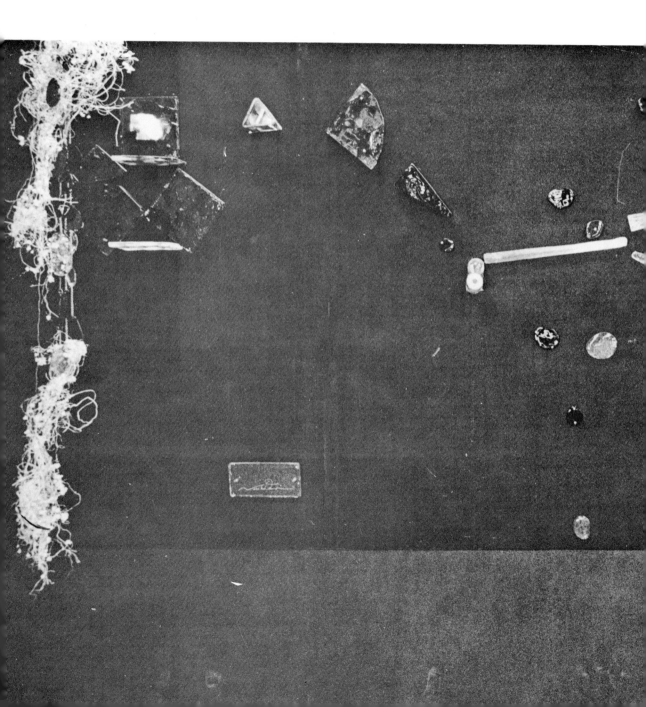

A Relief Ornament At The Entrance To A Department Store

Theme: Fantasy
Materials: crystal glass
Relief dimensions: width—4.5 meters, height—3 meters, weight—160 kilograms. Because I feel that women understand the pleasure of department stores better than men, employing the feeling of ikebana, I created a relief ornament that expresses the joy of shopping.

2. AN IKEBANA EXHIBITION

Having had much experience with exhibitions of ikebana, I am thoroughly convinced that they are of great emotional value to the designers themselves, as well as to the visitors who come to enjoy them. As you and your friends grow more proficient in the art of arrangement and want to hold exhibitions of your own, remember the following important points.

1. Determine the general emphasis of the entire exhibit first; then select a theme.
2. Pay close attention to the planning, color scheme, lighting and wall effects of the exhibition room.
3. Place each arrangement individually, giving thorough consideration to the level of proficiency of the arranger, the content, and the faithfulness to theme of each work.

Lighting from beneath made the arrangements seem to float. Throughout the display room carefully controlled ceiling lights produced a relaxing atmosphere.

At the entrance, a small wall of *oya* stone and a bridge added variety, and flower arrangements and mobiles hung from the ceiling gave a touch of actual movement. The multi-dimensional arrangement of the works, each placed so as to harmonize with its neighbors, seemed to engulf the large central column. In the whole diplay, variety within harmony was a main point.

In the center of the room, where the circular effect of the structure suggested a spiral, I set a large ceramic vase in gravel spread on the floor. In the vase I arranged a combination of anthurium from Hawaii, dried materials, and some black berries from Taiwan. The contrast between the bright pinks, reds, and whites of the anthurium and the somber colors of the dried materials and berries created a fascinating composition. Next to this exotic work I placed a roughly woven, Japanese bamboo basket with willow branches akebia, and fern in a representation of the worldwide desire for peace.

3. FLOWERS FOR A FASHION SHOW

In creating the important mood of lightness and fancy for a fashion show nothing is more effective than carefully selected and placed floral arrangements.

At the entrance, I used identical black vases filled with elegant orchids, bleached palm, dried berries, and dried mountain clover, added last to give a feeling of a blizzard of blossoms. The gaiety and charm of the arrangement set the mood for visitors on their way to the show.

Inside, where the fashions themselves are the important thing, there must be no distractions, but a few flowers highlight and enliven the tone of the stage. I selected a number of small suspended crystal globes filled with ivy and orchids. The rich purple of the flowers and the glittering glass and water gained tone and loveliness as they moved slowly in the currents of air.

4. FLOWERS AND POETRY

ARRANGEMENT FOR A DEPARTMENT
STORE WINDOW

A certain department store adopted
the policy of combining ikebana and
poetry to catch the eye of passing
patrons and to make them stop
to enjoy the mood for a moment.
Feeling that this was an excellent
opportunity to demonstrate the rela-
tionship between ikebana and poetry
and the joy the two combined can
bring into our lives, I poured a great

deal of affection into the arrangement
of such show windows as this one,
in which a floral relief (in circle)
focuses attention on the verses of the
French poet Guillaume Apollinaire.

A Demonstration In Holland

Held in Utrecht, under the sponsorship of the Holland Garden Association, this demonstration presented the traditional and modern aspects of ikebana to a thousand guests, both male and female. It was organized by Mrs. I.E. Knook, a member of the Holland Branch of International Ikebana, who since her visit to this country last year, has been actively promoting friendship and cultural exchange between her homeland and Japan.

Kokusai Ikebana Gakuin

L'international d'ikebana

13–16, 2-chome, Nakai, Shinjuku-ku, Tokyo, Japan
Tel. Tokyo (951) 4677

INDEX OF FLORAL MATERIALS